Why So Picky?

by S. E. Floyd

AuthorHouse™
1663 Liberty Drive
Bloomington, IN 47403
www.authorhouse.com
Phone: 833-262-8899

This book is printed on acid-free paper.

ISBN: 978-1-6655-3471-0 (sc)
978-1-6655-3472-7 (e)

Library of Congress Control Number: 2021916210

Print information available on the last page.

Published by AuthorHouse 08/13/2021

authorHOUSE®

Thank you to my wife Tangela and my mother Jackie Floyd for supporting my creative vibes. Bryson, Caleb and Zariah this book is dedicated to you. To God be the glory!

I brush my teeth in the morning.
My mom yells up the stairs ...

"Remember to brush your teeth!
Brush the front, back and sides!
Rinse and spit! Rinse and spit!"

MOM!!! WHY SO PICKY?

I put on my clothes to go to school. Dad yells ...

"Remember to tuck your shirt, zip your pants and wear a belt!"

I put on my shoes. Mom yells ...

"Remember, put your shoes on the right foot and tie your shoestrings tight so you won't fall!"

Why so picky !!!

I eat my breakfast. Mom and dad say,
"Remember, pray before you eat and
eat with your mouth closed."

Why so picky ?

I ride the bus to school. My seat
friend did not brush his teeth.

PEE-YOO!!!

I go to my classroom at school.
My teacher greets us at the door.

"Good morning! You look very neat with
your tucked shirt and belt", he said.

I SMILED.

I run and skip and jump on the playground.
My friend fell. His shoes were not tied tight.

I SMILE.

I eat lunch at school. My lunch friend
is eating with her mouth open.

Oops! She spilled food on her shirt. She should eat with her mouth closed.

I SMILE.

I go home after school. I hug my mom and dad. "How was your day?", mom asked.

I smile and hold mom and dad's hand.
"Thanks for being so picky", I said.

THE END

Printed in the United States
by Baker & Taylor Publisher Services